YOU CHOOSE BOOKS™

THE BOSTON MASSACRE

Revised Edition

An Interactive History Adventure

by Elizabeth Raum

Consultant:
Len Travers
Associate Professor of History
University of Massachusetts at Dartmouth

CAPSTONE PRESS
a capstone imprint

You Choose Books are published by Capstone Press,
1710 Roe Crest Drive, North Mankato, Minnesota 56003.
www.mycapstone.com

Library of Congress Cataloging-in-Publication Data is available on the Library of Congress website.
978-1-5157-4302-6 (revised hardcover)
978-1-5157-4261-6 (revised paperback)
978-1-5157-4374-3 (eBook pdf)
978-1-5157-4325-5 (eBook)

Editorial Credits
Angie Kaelberer, editor; Juliette Peters, set designer; Patrick D. Dentinger, book designer;
        Danielle Ceminsky, illustrator; Wanda Winch, photo researcher

Photo Credits
Alamy: Mary Evans Picture Library, 53, GL Archive, 74; Capstone Press: Danielle
Ceminsky, 9; Corbis: Bettmann, 35; Getty Images: Stock Montage, 55, 85; iStockphoto:
duncan1890, 16, 19; Library of Congress: 25, 33, 58, 90; New York Public Library/The
Miriam and Ira D. Wallach Division of Art, Prints and Photographs: Print Collection:
68, 105; North Wind Picture Archives, Cover, 6, 11, 12, 42, 44, 49, 63, 81, 95, 96, 100;
Shutterstock: Everett Historical, 41

Printed in China.
PO564

TABLE OF CONTENTS

ABOUT YOUR ADVENTURE

YOU are in Boston, Massachusetts, in 1770. For months, American colonists and British soldiers have been clashing in the city. Which side will you take?

In this book, you'll explore how the choices people made meant the difference between life and death. The events you'll experience happened to real people.

Chapter One sets the scene. Then you choose which path to read. Follow the directions at the bottom of each page. The choices you make will change your outcome. After you finish one path, go back and read the others for new perspectives and more adventures.

YOU CHOOSE the path
you take through history.

In late 1768, British soldiers in red coats marched through the streets of Boston.

Trouble in Boston

It's February 1770. The Province of
Massachusetts and 12 other colonies in North
America are under the rule of Great Britain.
People in the colonies still consider themselves
British. But many of them are tired of paying
high prices for goods imported from Britain.
They're also unhappy with the taxes they have
to pay to the British government.

In 1765, the British parliament passed
the Stamp Act. This law put a tax on every
document, newspaper, and pamphlet printed
in the colonies.

7

Turn the page.

In Boston, Massachusetts, a group of shopkeepers and craftsmen organized to fight the Stamp Act. They called themselves the Loyal Nine. The Loyal Nine convinced Bostonians to gather in the streets to protest the tax. The violent protests were enough to make Parliament repeal the tax in 1766.

Later, the Loyal Nine changed their name to the Sons of Liberty. Their members included silversmith Paul Revere, politician and writer Samuel Adams, and shipowner John Hancock. The group met under the Liberty Tree. This giant elm was about a block east of Boston Common park. The Sons of Liberty told Bostonians not to do business with merchants who traded with the British.

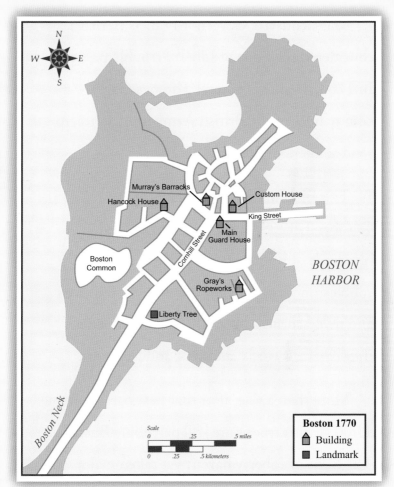

Murray's Barracks

Hancock House

Custom House

King Street

Main
Guard House

Cornhill Street

Boston
Common

BOSTON
HARBOR

Gray's
Ropeworks

Liberty Tree

Boston Neck

Scale
0   .25   .5 miles

0   .25   .5 kilometers

Boston 1770

Building

Landmark

Turn the page.

Massachusetts Governor Francis Bernard considered the Sons of Liberty troublemakers. In 1768, he asked General Thomas Gage, commander of the British Army in America, to send soldiers to Boston.

The 14th and 29th regiments arrived October 1, 1768. Soon after they arrived, hundreds of soldiers paraded through the cobblestone streets. They wore bright red coats and three-cornered black hats. At their sides, they carried swords, muskets, and bayonets.

More than a year after that first parade, about 4,000 British troops are still patrolling Boston. The Sons of Liberty haven't yet taken major action against them. But tensions are building, and Boston is in the midst of trouble.

Groups of colonists met to protest the taxes the British government required them to pay.

➤ To be a 13-year-old apprentice in Boston, turn to page **13**.

➤ To serve as a British soldier in Boston, turn to page **45**.

➤ To experience the events as John Hancock's maid, turn to page **69**.

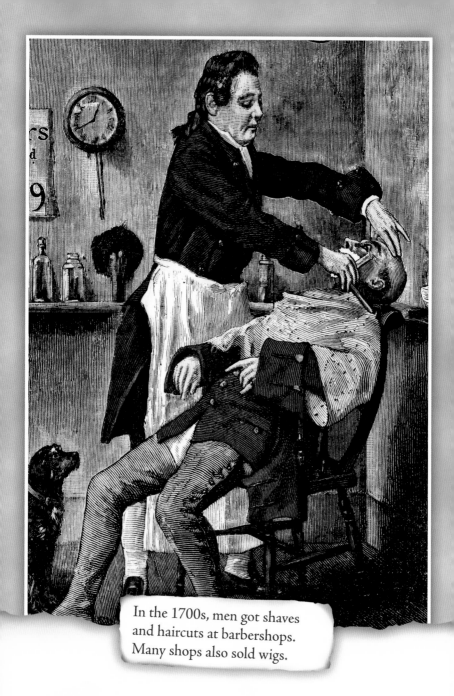

In the 1700s, men got shaves and haircuts at barbershops. Many shops also sold wigs.

CHAPTER 2

The Wigmaker's Apprentice

You roll the measuring tape into a neat coil, put the curling irons away, and sweep the powdery floor. Mr. John Piemont insists that his barbershop be kept neat and in order. At 13, you are the youngest and newest apprentice, so the job falls to you.

As an apprentice, you also make deliveries. One day, Mr. Piemont asks you to deliver a wig to Mrs. Grizzell Apthorp's house. You get hopelessly lost. You've lived in Boston only three months. With nearly 16,000 people, Boston is much bigger than the town of Framingham, where you grew up.

Turn the page.

"Are you lost?" a boy asks you.

"I'm afraid so," you reply. "I'm looking for Mrs. Apthorp's house."

He laughs. "Come with me. I work for the lady. My name's Christopher Seider."

Chris is a year or two younger than you. On the way to Mrs. Apthorp's home, you become friends. "Come back whenever you have some time off. If I'm free, I'll show you around town," he says.

You deliver the wig and return to Piemont's. In quiet moments, the older apprentices tell you about a group many of them belong to. "We're called the Sons of Liberty because we fight for liberty," one apprentice says.

"Yes," another says. "If a merchant sells imported British goods, we teach him a lesson. We smear tar on his windows, destroy his garden, and mark up his signs."

It sounds like trouble to you, but you admire their spirit. One day, you wander past the Liberty Tree, a giant elm. "It's more than 120 years old," an apprentice tells you. "The Sons of Liberty meet under it. When someone gives us a hard time, we make a dummy that looks like the person. Then we hang it from a branch of the Liberty Tree with a sign around its neck."

"We call it an effigy," another apprentice adds. "It's a warning."

You feel a shiver of excitement. These boys are part of something important.

Turn the page.

Protesters sometimes hung dummies called effigies from the branches of the Liberty Tree.

Mr. Piemont gives you a few hours off on the morning of February 22. Another apprentice, John, invites you to walk with him to Boston Neck. This strip of land connects Boston to the mainland. But then you remember Christopher Seider had invited you to visit him the next time you were free.

→ To go with John, turn to page **18**.

→ To meet Chris Seider, turn to page **20**.

Once you reach Boston Neck, you see an army guard on duty. John walks up to the guard and starts yelling. "Hey, lobster back!" he shouts. You and John have a good laugh as you call the guard names. But it's cold, so you soon leave.

The next day, you arrive at work to find all of the other apprentices working silently. Their faces are pale and serious. "What's wrong?" you ask.

John answers, "Yesterday, Ebenezer Richardson killed the boy who works for Mrs. Apthorp. Christopher Seider was his name."

"How did it happen?" you cry.

"A mob attacked Theophilus Lillie for importing British goods. Richardson came to his aid. He fired his musket into the crowd," another apprentice, Edward Garrick, says.

"I knew Chris," you whisper. What if you'd been there? Could you have saved him?

Christopher Seider was shot in front of Theophilus Lillie's shop.

Samuel Adams is organizing a funeral for Chris. All of the apprentices want to go, but someone has to help in the shop.

*To go the funeral, turn to page 23.

To stay behind to work, turn to page 24.

You find Christopher hauling charcoal near Mrs. Apthorp's house. You hear people shouting from the street. "What's going on?" you ask him.

A crowd tosses rocks at a nearby house, breaking windows. Chris tells you it's Ebenezer Richardson's home. "He's a tax collector for the British. He tried to stop a Sons of Liberty protest. Now they're teaching him a lesson."

A man tosses a bat through a window. Richardson appears at one of the broken windows. He aims a musket at the crowd. "Stand off, or I'll fire," he yells.

Chris bends down to pick up a stone. "No, Chris!" you yell. But it's too late. Richardson pulls the trigger, and Chris crumples to the ground. Several men pick him up and carry him away.

➤ To follow the men, go to page 21.
➤ To return to Piemont's, turn to page 22.

You follow the men carrying Chris to a nearby house. Maybe he's not hurt too badly. Maybe he'll be fine once he rests for a bit.

No one stops you as you enter the house. The men place Chris on a bed. A doctor rushes past you. "Where's the boy?" he shouts, and you point to the bed.

The doctor bends over Chris. "It's serious," he says. "You all need to leave now."

You leave quietly. There is nothing you can do to help. You pray that Chris will recover as you head back to the barbershop.

Turn the page.

You return to Piemont's. Later that night, you're sad to hear the news that Chris died. All the apprentices are talking about the funeral that Samuel Adams is planning.

"Samuel Adams is Boston's leading patriot," Edward Garrick says. "He writes articles for the newspaper about the way Parliament is mistreating us here in the colonies." Several apprentices are going to Chris' funeral, but someone has to stay and watch the shop.

➺To go to the funeral, go to page 23.

➺To stay at work, turn to page 24.

The funeral is February 26. You join hundreds of other boys walking ahead of Chris' casket through the streets of Boston. After the burial, you hurry back to the shop. If you keep busy, maybe you won't think about your friend's death.

A British soldier from the 29th Regiment, Patrick Dines, works at Piemont's shop in his spare time. You like Dines. He's a good fellow, even though he's a soldier.

After work on Monday, March 5, Dines invites several of the apprentices to visit his barracks. You're curious to see the barracks, but will going there mean you support the soldiers? Edward Garrick invites you to walk around town. "Maybe we can stir up a little trouble," he says.

➤To go to the barracks, turn to page **26**.

➤To walk around town, turn to page **27**.

You feel as if you should go to the funeral, but you're too upset. You spend the day working silently in the shop. You try not to think about Chris, but it's hard.

After the funeral, another apprentice tells you that there were at least 2,000 people there. That number included 400 schoolboys, who marched ahead of the casket.

One day in early March, several soldiers come by for shaves. When they leave, Mr. Piemont says that Captain John Goldfinch owes him money. "If you can collect it, you can keep it," he tells Edward Garrick.

It snows on Monday, March 5. By evening, the weather is clear, but the roads are still icy. "I'm off to see what's going on in the streets," Edward says. "Want to join me?"

During the 1770s, Boston's streets were places to meet friends and gather news.

Just then, another apprentice, Bartholomew Broaders, comes in. He says that Mr. Green, who lives in the Custom House, asked him to walk with his daughter, Ann, and her friend. They're headed to the apothecary to pick up medicine. "Want to come with us?" Bartholomew asks you.

➤ *To go with Edward, turn to page 27.*

➤ *To go with Bartholomew, turn to page 30.*

You and two other boys go to the barracks with Dines. He shows you around as you talk to the soldiers of the 29th. You are about to leave when you overhear Sergeant Daniels say, "We've put up with the insults of these Bostonians long enough. It's time to show them who's in charge."

When you return to your lodgings, apprentice Edward Garrick says he's going out. "If there's a fight, I want to be there. You should come too."

You sneeze. Your head feels fuzzy. "I'm catching a cold. Maybe I'll stay in."

"Come with me to the apothecary," apprentice Bartholomew Broaders says. "Mr. Green, who lives in the Custom House, asked me to walk his daughter and her friend there. They'll have medicines if you feel sick."

→To go with Edward, go to page 27.
→To join Bartholomew, turn to page 30.

You and Edward walk down Cornhill Street to the Main Guard building. Across King Street, a single soldier stands at a sentry post in front of the Custom House.

While you are standing there, Captain John Goldfinch walks by. You remember that Mr. Piemont said Goldfinch owed him money. "There goes the fellow who won't pay Mr. Piemont for fixing his hair," Edward shouts. Goldfinch ignores Edward and keeps walking down the street.

Just then, Bartholomew Broaders, Ann Green, and her friend Molly Rogers arrive. They invite you and Edward inside the Custom House.

As you talk in the Custom House, you hear shouts from outside. Edward and Bartholomew want to go out and see what's going on. But you think it might be safer to stay inside.

➤To go outside, turn to page 28.

➤To stay inside, turn to page 31.

As you walk out of the Custom House, Edward begins complaining about Goldfinch again. The guard at the post, Private Hugh White, overhears him. "Goldfinch is a gentleman," he protests.

"There's not a gentleman in the entire regiment," Edward says.

White steps out from his post. "Let me see your face."

"I'm not ashamed to show my face," Edward says. As Edward juts out his chin, White swings his musket. It strikes Edward in the head.

"Ouch!" Edward yells in pain.

"Why did you do that?" you shout at White. "He didn't do anything to you!" You and Bartholomew pick up pebbles and pieces of ice and hurl them at White.

Suddenly, church bells begin to ring. Usually, that's a fire alarm. People begin pouring into the square to fight the fire.

"This soldier attacked my friend for no reason at all!" you shout to the growing crowd.

"Lousy rascal! Redcoat!" The crowd shouts insults and hurls rocks at White. White raises his musket. "If they attack me, I will fire," he says.

"Let's get out of here," you say to Edward.

"Go ahead if you want," he replies. "But I'm not leaving."

➻To stay with Edward, turn to page **32**.

➻To go back to your lodgings, turn to page **39**.

As you walk with Bartholomew and the girls, groups of soldiers pass you. You also see a group of club-carrying townspeople. You walk faster. When you reach the Custom House, Edward is there. You all decide to go inside.

As you talk with your friends, you hear noises from the streets outside. "Let's go see what's going on," Edward says.

"I don't think that's a good idea," you reply. "I'm staying here." Edward and Bartholomew slip out the front door.

You don't want to be in the middle of the action, but you still want to see what's happening. You and the girls walk upstairs and look out the window at the street below. There's a British soldier standing at a sentry post in front of the Custom House.

From the window, you see Edward and Bartholomew arguing with the sentry. A crowd gathers around them. Some soldiers come to help the sentry, but the crowd won't let them move.

Suddenly, you hear a gunshot. More shots follow. Several men fall into the street, bleeding. You slip back to your lodgings. There you hear that 11 men were shot, and at least three died. Edward and Bartholomew weren't hurt.

The next day, one of the Sons of Liberty asks you what happened at the Custom House. "We have a report that shots were fired from inside. It will help our cause if we have a witness who saw the soldiers firing from that location," he tells you.

You want to help, but you know soldiers weren't inside the Custom House. And you didn't see the shots being fired.

→ To tell the truth, turn to page 36.

→ To lie, turn to page 37.

Edward might need your help. You stay. Edward's moans stir up the crowd. They throw sticks and stones at the guard.

A mob comes up the street swinging bats and clubs. A large, dark-skinned man armed with a club leads the group. "That's Crispus Attucks," someone says. "And there's Sam Gray," another adds. "He fought with some soldiers at the ropeworks on Friday."

More people pour into King Street. Some carry buckets to fight what they believe is a fire. Others carry bats, swords, or clubs. One man rips the leg off a market stand to use as a weapon. You stand in the middle of the crowd, unsure of what to do.

Private White calls for help. "Turn out the Main Guard!"

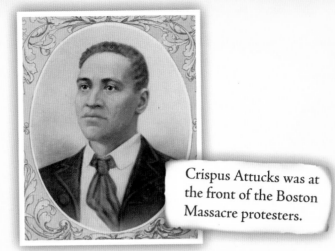

Crispus Attucks was at the front of the Boston Massacre protesters.

Captain Thomas Preston arrives with a small group of soldiers. As they try to cross King Street, they disappear into the crowd. They finally reach White at his post.

White falls in with the other soldiers. Preston tries to march them back to the Main Guard building. But the crowd blocks them. "Fire!" the townspeople yell at the soldiers. "Fire your guns!"

You turn away, ready to run. "Don't be afraid, lad," a man says to you. "They dare not fire."

Then a gun goes off. Boom!

Turn the page.

The crowd pushes toward Royal Exchange Lane and down King Street. You have no choice but to flee with them. As you look back, you see several coats lying in the snow. Then you realize that they aren't coats. They are the bodies of the men shot by the British soldiers.

You feel sick. You've lost track of Edward and Bartholomew. Are they among the dead?

When you get back to your lodgings, the other boys are already there. You sigh with relief, but your heart is heavy. Eleven men were shot, and at least three died. Your taunts may have been partly to blame. Edward says that it was bound to happen. You only tossed pebbles and ice. The soldiers were the ones with guns.

The next day, some of the Sons of Liberty stop by the barbershop. They want to take statements from everyone who saw the shootings.

The bodies of the victims looked like coats tossed into the snowy street.

You're not sure if you saw enough to give an accurate account.

➤ To give a statement, turn to page **38**.

➤ To refuse, turn to page **40**.

You give an honest account of the shooting. When asked if anyone shot a gun out of the windows of the Custom House, you say no. Even though others disagree, you don't change your story.

At first, you are afraid that the Sons of Liberty will call you a traitor, but that never happens. Maybe that's what freedom is about. You are free to tell the truth as you see it. You feel calm and believe the whole truth will come out in the trial.

THE END

To follow another path, turn to page 11.
To read the conclusion, turn to page 101.

You say that soldiers fired from the windows of the Custom House. After all, it's important that the soldiers are punished.

But by the end of the week, you realize that you can't live with telling a lie. You find the man who took your testimony and confess.

"The truth will come out at the trial," he says. "They probably won't even call on you to testify, but we wanted to get as many accounts as we could. Some were accurate, but there may have been others like yours — people who stretched the truth a bit to serve the cause. I thank you for being a true Son of Liberty."

You can't help but smile. You are a patriot. When you are older, you'll fight for liberty.

THE END

To follow another path, turn to page 11.
To read the conclusion, turn to page 101.

You try to give an honest account. You are certain the captain said, "Fire!" Samuel Adams writes about the shootings in the *Boston Gazette*. He calls it the Boston Massacre. Paul Revere prints an engraving that shows soldiers firing into an unarmed crowd. Maybe he was there that night, but you never saw him.

After a while, you forget what you actually saw. You are convinced that whatever happened was the soldiers' fault. They'll go to trial. Even with famous lawyers John Adams and Josiah Quincy defending them, they'll probably be found guilty. You expect to see them hanged on Boston Common.

THE END

To follow another path, turn to page 11.
To read the conclusion, turn to page 101.

You return to your lodgings and get ready for bed. But you can't fall asleep. You're worried about Edward and Bartholomew.

Several hours later, the other boys slip into the room. As Edward lights a candle, you see that his face is pale. "What happened after I left?" you ask him.

"The Redcoats fired on the crowd," Edward replies. "Eleven men were shot. Sam Gray was killed. So was Crispus Attucks. I'm not sure about the rest."

The next day, the soldiers are arrested. Once the soldier's trials are over, you hope Boston will be peaceful again.

THE END

To follow another path, turn to page 11.
To read the conclusion, turn to page 101.

"I'd like to help," you say, "but I didn't see exactly what happened."

The men talk to other apprentices. A few days later, you meet one of the men in the street. "You're the boy who wanted to help, aren't you?" he asks.

You nod. He hands you a pile of printed handbills. "This is an engraving Paul Revere made of the Boston Massacre. You can help our cause by dropping these off at shops and handing them out all over town. We want everyone to know what happened on March 5, 1770."

As he walks away, you look at Mr. Revere's picture of British soldiers shooting into a helpless crowd. This is not what you saw. The townspeople had clubs and bats. They were throwing ice, shells, and dirt. Should you help distribute a picture that you know isn't accurate?

Paul Revere made an engraving of the Boston Massacre, based on a drawing by Henry Pelham.

⟶ To distribute the handbills, turn to page **42**.

⟶ To toss them, turn to page **43**.

You distribute the handbills. A picture like this is bound to convince people that the British soldiers must leave the colonies. Does it really matter whether or not the picture is accurate?

Paul Revere and other patriots distributed handbills showing his engraving of the massacre.

THE END

To follow another path, turn to page 11.
To read the conclusion, turn to page 101.

You hide the handbills under your coat and return to work. Later, you slip the bills under a loose floorboard. No one will ever know that you didn't distribute them. People believe what they see on paper, even if it's wrong. You'll find better ways to help the cause of liberty.

THE END

To follow another path, turn to page 11.
To read the conclusion, turn to page 101.

Boston schoolboys sometimes taunted and threw things at the British soldiers.

CHAPTER 3

A King's Soldier in Boston

"Redcoat!" a young boy yells. "Bloodyback!" Another boy hurls a rock along with his insults.

You duck just in time. In the last few months, people have tossed stones, dirt, ice, and snowballs at you as you walk the streets of Boston.

You'd like to knock some sense into the boys, but you can't. You're a soldier in the king's army. Your job is to protect the people of Boston. It wouldn't be right to strike out at them, even though they deserve it.

Turn the page.

Some of your fellow soldiers are letting the tension get to them. One had too much to drink one night and rode his horse into a family's parlor. Instead of being embarrassed, the soldier just laughed and rode back outside.

Some soldiers hold target practice outside churches on Sunday mornings to disturb the people inside. Others tease ladies on their way to market or steal apples from farmers' carts. It seems childish to you, but you understand why they've decided to fight back. You're all tired of being the enemy. When you see farmers coming to town on market day, you think about what a good life they must have.

One November day in 1769, you go to Piemont's Barbershop for a shave. As you leave the shop, a man comes up to you. You've seen him before. He's always been friendly and respectful.

"May I have a word, sir?" he asks. When you agree, he pulls you into a side alley.

"I have an opportunity for you," he says. "There are some of us here in Boston who know you are not the enemy. Have you given any thought to staying here in the colonies?" He offers to help you settle in America if you'll desert the British Army.

You're tempted. There's nothing for you in Britain. Your family is poor, and the life of a soldier is hard. The army pays very little. If you stay, you might be able to become a farmer. But you'll be a deserter. The army hangs deserters. "We'll protect you," the man says. Can he?

→To stay in the army, turn to page **48**.

→To desert, turn to page **50**.

You say no to the man's offer. Deserters deserve to hang. You do wish the army paid better, though. To earn extra money, you take a job unloading cargo from ships in the harbor.

You are in the barracks on the afternoon of Friday, March 2, 1770. Patrick Walker returns from Gray's Ropeworks. His face is red with anger. "What happened?" you ask.

"I was looking for work," he says. "But instead, I was insulted and knocked down, just because I'm a soldier. Go back to the ropeworks with me. We'll get even."

You, Walker, and eight or nine other soldiers arrive at the ropeworks ready to fight. But in the meantime, the ropeworkers called for their friends, who showed up with clubs. You don't stand a chance against so many. You return to the barracks to get more soldiers.

Soldiers and other single men often ate their meals at taverns.

Once you are back at the barracks, you have second thoughts. What's the point of making the brawl worse? Maybe you'll go to the tavern instead. The owner's wife cooks a fine stew. Just thinking about it makes you hungry.

➤To go to the tavern, turn to page **51**.

➤To join the fight, turn to page **52**.

"Yes," you say. "I'll accept your offer and leave the army."

"Then it's settled. We can hide you here in Boston. You're one of us now."

But there's another choice. The man offers you the chance to go to Rhode Island. "There's a wealthy man there, a friend of liberty, who will give you a small plot of land to farm."

➤To stay in Boston, turn to page **56**.

➤To move to Rhode Island, turn to page **62**.

You have supper at the tavern and then return to your barracks. Several bruised soldiers stagger back from the ropeworks. It's clear that the ropeworkers won this round.

On the evening of Monday, March 5, you plan to return to the tavern. But several soldiers ask you to join them in a walk around town. "Trouble's brewing. We plan to show the townspeople who's in charge."

It sounds like another foolish fight. But at some point you'll have to deal with these rebellious Bostonians.

➤*To go to the tavern, turn to page 54.*

➤*To join the soldiers, turn to page 57.*

At the ropeworks, you fight with a mob of ropeworkers and others who work in the area. There are too many of them for you to win the fight. After returning to the barracks to ask more soldiers to help, you try again. But once again, the workers have the upper hand.

On Saturday, three of your fellow soldiers go back to the ropeworks. During the fight that follows, Private John Rodgers suffers a broken arm and a cracked skull. This news makes you even angrier. But you won't be able to do anything about it tomorrow. Sunday is for attending church services, not fighting.

"Wait until Monday night," a soldier says. "We'll settle this once and for all."

"I wish I could go with you," you say, but you have guard duty that evening. Your shift follows that of Private Hugh White.

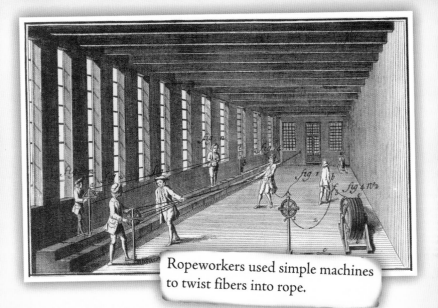

Ropeworkers used simple machines to twist fibers into rope.

On Monday night, you are polishing your musket in the barracks. You hear White shout, "Turn out, Main Guard!" Church bells begin clanging. That usually means there's a fire.

"Turn out, Main Guard!" White calls again.

Captain Thomas Preston shouts, "I need men to help White at the sentry post."

➤*To volunteer to help White, turn to page* **59**.

➤*To wait, turn to page* **64**.

You go to the tavern and notice groups of soldiers and townspeople in the streets. Church bells begin to ring. Is it a fire alarm? People rush from houses carrying buckets. You run out into the street.

"Where's the fire?" you ask a man.

"There's no fire. It's a riot."

In front of the Custom House, five or six soldiers stand in a semicircle, holding their guns. A crowd yells insults and tosses rocks and pieces of ice at the soldiers. You circle behind the crowd toward your barracks.

Someone yells, "Fire!"

Boom! A shot rings out.

You run toward the barracks. An armed soldier brushes past you, kneels down, and points his gun at the townspeople.

In the confusion, no one was sure who gave the order to shoot.

"Stop," an officer yells at him. "Don't shoot!"

The soldier doesn't put down his musket. The officer turns to you. "Take away his gun!" he yells at you.

"Don't touch me!" the soldier with the musket says. He swings his gun in your direction.

➤ To stop the soldier, turn to page 66.

➤ To leave him alone, turn to page 67.

"I'll stay in Boston," you say. You leave your barracks one day and never return. For several weeks, you live in a shopkeeper's attic. The shopkeeper is a member of the Sons of Liberty.

After a month of hiding, you take a job on a fishing boat. One day on shore, you notice a man watching you. The man looks familiar. He's not in uniform. Is he from your former regiment?

That night, you mention the stranger to the shopkeeper. "He could be an army agent," he says. "Maybe you should leave. We have friends in Rhode Island who would gladly take you in."

You like Boston and working on the fishing boat. Most of the time, the boat is out to sea. You're safe then. But are you safe enough?

➻To go to Rhode Island, turn to page 62.

➻To stay in Boston, turn to page 65.

You join a group of soldiers walking through Draper's Alley to Cornhill Street and onto Brattle Street. A large crowd of townspeople with clubs and sticks pound on buildings along the streets and alleyways. They are noisy, but you don't think they are dangerous.

But when you return to the barracks, a mob is waiting. People in the crowd throw snow, ice, and oyster shells at you. You cover your head as officers hustle you and the other soldiers inside.

Later that night, you hear that the soldiers shot 11 civilians in front of the Custom House. Three died at the scene. "They've arrested Captain Preston and eight soldiers," an officer tells you.

"They would never shoot into an unarmed crowd," you say.

Turn the page.

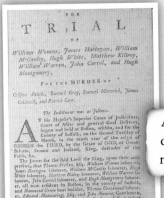

A poster listed the names of the soldiers tried for the murders of the civilians.

"The crowd was armed, all right — with clubs, sticks, and swords," the officer says. "But since they didn't have guns, there will be a trial. I doubt it will be fair."

58

You nod, relieved that you didn't have to face the crowd. Maybe now you'll be sent home. You've seen enough of America to last a lifetime.

THE END

To follow another path, turn to page 11.
To read the conclusion, turn to page 101.

You are one of six privates who go to White's aid. Captain Preston and Corporal William Wemms march beside you. You carry a musket. It's unloaded, but it has a fixed bayonet. When the crowd begins pushing, you use the bayonet to lightly jab anyone who gets too close.

You load your musket when you reach the sentry box. Preston orders White to join your formation. Preston then orders all of you to march back to the Main Guard.

But the crowd presses too close. You can't move. You form a semicircle as you stand a body-width apart from one another. Preston is in front of you. "Go home," he yells to the crowd.

People pelt him with snowballs and insults. "Fire!" the crowd yells. "Fire your guns!"

Turn the page.

It's a dare. Your finger itches to pull the trigger, but Preston told you not to fire. You tremble, both in anger and fear.

Someone throws a club at Private Hugh Montgomery, knocking him down. Boom! Private Montgomery's gun goes off.

"Fire!" someone yells. Is it Preston? It must be.

You shoot into the crowd. More shots roar from the muskets of the other soldiers.

"Stop firing!" It's Captain Preston. You put down your gun.

When the crowd clears, you see bodies in the street. Four? Five?

"What have we done?" you whisper in horror. Men are dead. Were they armed? Did they fire?

Preston marches you back to the Main Guard. He calls out the entire guard and positions groups of soldiers along King Street. You are prepared for another attack. But it never comes. The crowd leaves, and you return to the barracks.

You can't sleep. You are still awake at 2:00 in the morning when Sheriff Stephen Greenleaf comes to arrest Captain Preston.

Early that morning, you and the other seven soldiers turn yourselves in to the authorities. You shiver in your jail cell. There will be a trial. If you're found guilty, you could be sentenced to die. You hope that the colonists will treat you fairly and set you free.

THE END

To follow another path, turn to page 11.
To read the conclusion, turn to page 101.

You take the offer to move to Tiverton, Rhode Island. At first, you help the landowner farm his land. In time, the town gives you your own piece of land. You join the local Sons of Liberty.

In March 1770, you hear bad news from Boston. A dispute between British soldiers and townspeople ended with 11 colonists being shot. Five of them died. You're glad you left Boston and weren't involved.

In April 1775, the Revolutionary War begins between Great Britain and the colonists. You help the patriot cause as a drill leader of the local militia. These soldiers will be aiming their guns at men who used to be your countrymen. You hope that the fight ends quickly without too many losses on either side.

Members of colonial militias fought against British soldiers during the Revolutionary War.

THE END

To follow another path, turn to page 11.
To read the conclusion, turn to page 101.

You remain in the barracks. You hear the angry shouts of the mob, followed by musket blasts. Later that night, one of the men who had gone with Preston says, "We had no choice. If we hadn't shot into the crowd, they would have killed us."

Captain Preston is arrested very early the next morning. A few hours later, the eight soldiers who were with him turn themselves in to the authorities. Within a few days, the rest of the soldiers in Boston are moved to Castle William. This fort is on Castle Island, 3 miles from shore in Boston Harbor. By the time the trials begin, you are off on another mission for the king.

THE END

To follow another path, turn to page 11.
To read the conclusion, turn to page 101.

A few days later, as you eat supper with the shopkeeper and his family, the door bursts open. You're horrified to see a British army captain and several soldiers standing there.

The man you saw at the docks was a British agent. He reported you to the army commander.

"You are under arrest for desertion," the captain roars.

Soldiers drag you off to the barracks. Two days later, they march you to Boston Common. You die with a noose around your neck.

THE END

To follow another path, turn to page 11.
To read the conclusion, turn to page 101.

You knock the soldier's gun aside before he can fire. You and the officer grab the soldier and push him inside the barracks.

The next day, you hear soldiers shot 11 townspeople in front of the Custom House. Three of them died at the scene. Nine soldiers are arrested and will be tried for murder.

A few days later, you are shipped to Castle William, a fort on an island in Boston Harbor. From there, you are sent back to Great Britain. There, you wait for news of the soldiers' trials. You hope that their lives will be spared.

THE END

To follow another path, turn to page 11.
To read the conclusion, turn to page 101.

You stand aside. The soldier raises his gun. Before he can fire, the officer knocks him over from behind. "Help me get him inside," the officer tells you.

You take one of the man's arms while the officer takes the other. You march the soldier to the barracks.

Later that night, you hear that the soldiers in front of the Custom House did fire on the crowd. Eleven men were shot, and three died at the scene. The nine soldiers accused of shooting them will be tried for murder.

A few days later, your regiment leaves Boston. You say a silent goodbye to your fellow soldiers in prison. You hope they will get fair trials.

THE END

To follow another path, turn to page 11.
To read the conclusion, turn to page 101.

John Hancock was one of Boston's most famous merchants and patriots.

CHAPTER 4

The Maid's Story

You wake before sunrise. It's hard to get out of bed on these cold February mornings. But it's your job to light the fires. First, you light the kitchen fireplace. Then you tiptoe throughout Mr. John Hancock's big house. You stir the embers in each fireplace and add wood so that the house will be toasty by daybreak.

Mr. Hancock's house sits high atop Beacon Hill, surrounded by elegant gardens. After all, Mr. Hancock is one of Boston's leaders. His ships carry goods all around the world.

Turn the page.

"You'll be amazed who comes here to meet with Mr. Hancock," Cook said when you came to work at the big house. "Many of the leaders of the Sons of Liberty — Paul Revere, Samuel Adams, and Will Molineux. Remember, what happens in this house stays in this house. Don't wag your tongue in the streets of Boston. If you can't keep a secret, you don't belong here."

Now that you've been here several months, Cook trusts you. She lumbers into the kitchen and puts on a pot of water to boil. "We're nearly out of Labrador tea," she says. "Oh, how I miss real English tea."

There's been no real tea for some time now. The Sons of Liberty won't allow it, because tea is imported from Britain. Labrador tea is made from a bush. It's a poor substitute for real tea, but Cook would never disobey Mr. Hancock.

"After you get the tea, go to Mr. Revere's shop. He's made a fine silver bowl for Mr. Hancock."

Cook warns you to be careful. Newspaper reports tell of British soldiers bothering girls and women, beating up boys, and causing all sorts of trouble.

You stop to watch the cows grazing on Boston Common. They remind you of your home, a farm near Lexington, Massachusetts. Today, February 22, is your brother's birthday. Even though you enjoy life in the big city, you miss your family.

There's a commotion in the street near Mr. Revere's shop. One of his apprentices rushes past. "Come quick," he says. "It's Mr. Theophilus Lillie. He imports and sells goods from Britain. Some of the boys plan to teach him a lesson."

➤ To join the crowd, turn to page 72.

➤ To pick up the bowl and go home, turn to page 74.

You dash after the apprentice. The street is filled with people. They are blocking the entrance to Mr. Lillie's shop. The windows of the shop are covered with tar and feathers. Several schoolboys are hurling rocks at the shop. A sign on a post has a hand pointing to Lillie's shop. Below the hand is the word "importer."

A man in a wagon tries to knock down the sign. As the man jumps from the wagon and runs down the street, the boys follow him. They throw clumps of dirt, sticks, and stones at him before he disappears into his house.

"That's Ebenezer Richardson," the apprentice tells you. "He's a tax collector."

A man tosses a bat through Richardson's window. "Ouch!" cries a woman inside. The boys continue to throw rocks. Then Richardson appears at one of the broken windows.

"Stand off or I'll fire," Richardson yells. He points a musket at the crowd. One look at his face tells you that he is serious. You know you should slip through a back alley to safety. But you want to see what will happen next.

→To stay, turn to page **76**.

→To slip away, turn to page **80**.

Paul Revere was famous for creating bowls and other objects from silver.

There's enough trouble in Boston without looking for more. You stop at Revere's shop to pick up the bowl and then head home.

You are in the kitchen helping Cook when one of the stablehands rushes into the house. "There was a shooting in front of Ebenezer Richardson's house," he says. "A boy was shot. He'll likely die."

"A boy?" Cook says, wringing her hands. "Samuel Adams said that all Boston needs is a spark, and it will explode in violence." Is this the spark?

The next day, you learn that Richardson wounded two men and killed 11-year-old Christopher Seider. "They are planning a big funeral, starting near the Liberty Tree," Cook says. "You can go if you want, but I'll stay here and watch the house. With these soldiers running wild, I'm afraid they might damage Mr. Hancock's property."

→To go to the funeral, turn to page 83.

→To watch the house, turn to page 86.

You stay to see what happens.

Richardson fires into the crowd. A young boy standing beside you tumbles forward. Blood oozes from his chest and stomach. He's just a boy, only 11 or 12 years old. How could such a thing happen?

You reach out to help him, but several men rush forward, lift the boy, and carry him home. Maybe you could help.

→*To follow the men, go to page 77.*

→*To return to Mr. Hancock's house, turn to page 79.*

The men carry the boy to a nearby house. You are about to go in when a doctor rushes past you. "Where is the boy?" he shouts as he disappears into the dark house.

"Who are you?" a woman at the door asks.

"I saw what happened," you stammer. "I thought maybe I could help."

"You'd best be going along now. The doctor will take charge. Christopher is in no condition to see anyone."

You don't say a word about the shooting to Cook when you return. You enjoy running errands. If Cook thought you were in danger, she'd never let you out again.

Turn the page.

The next morning, Cook says, "Mr. Hancock says Ebenezer Richardson shot and killed a boy yesterday. He wounded two men as well."

"The boy died?" you gasp.

"What's wrong?" Cook asks. "You're as pale as a peeled potato."

"He was standing beside me," you say. "He was as close as you are."

Cook puts an arm around your shoulders. "These are bad times," she says. "We have to be extra careful now. Mr. Hancock says there's to be a big funeral for the boy. You should go. It helps to mourn."

"You're right," you reply. "I'll go to the funeral and pay my respects."

Turn to page 83.

You flee to the safety of Mr. Hancock's house and tell no one what you have seen. You're afraid that Cook will send someone else on errands if she finds out the truth.

Cook tells you later that the boy, Christopher Seider, died. The Sons of Liberty are organizing a huge funeral for Monday afternoon, February 26. Mr. Hancock encourages everyone in his household to go. But a few must stay to watch the house. Cook fears that the soldiers will cause trouble.

→To go to the funeral, turn to page **83**.

→To stay home, turn to page **86**.

You turn and dash into the alley. You are almost into the next street when the bell of the New Brick Church on Hanover Street begins to toll. A crowd surges through the alley, forcing you back toward Richardson's house. You watch as men grab Richardson.

"What happened?" you ask.

"Richardson fired into the crowd, wounding two men and a boy. The boy's badly hurt. They say he's dying."

A man appears with a noose. He ties it on a signpost. "Hang him," the crowd calls.

"Stop!" Will Molineux steps forward. "You can't take justice into your own hands!" he shouts to the crowd. "Take Richardson to a judge and make sure he has a proper trial."

John Hancock's elegant house was located in the Beacon Hill neighborhood.

Reluctantly, the men agree. As the mob drags Richardson off in one direction, you head back to Mr. Hancock's house. You're relieved. You didn't want to witness a hanging.

Turn the page.

In the *Boston Gazette*, Samuel Adams reports that 11-year-old Christopher Seider was the victim of Richardson's gunfire. He organizes a funeral for Seider and invites all "friends of liberty" to attend.

You consider yourself a friend of liberty, so you plan to go. But Cook asks you to stay and help guard the house. She worries that soldiers will destroy Mr. Hancock's property if no one is home.

➤*To go to the funeral, go to page* **83**.

➤*To stay home, turn to page* **86**.

You've never seen such a big funeral parade. It begins at the Seider home just beyond the Liberty Tree. About 2,000 people attend the funeral service. At least 400 schoolboys walk ahead of the casket.

Friday, March 2, is your day off. Your friend Sarah invites you to go for a walk.

"Let's go down to the South End to Mr. John Gray's Ropeworks," Sarah says. "I want you to meet my boyfriend, Sam Gray. He works there."

Boston has several ropeworks. These places make and repair the ropes used on ships. You and Sarah walk down Pearl Street and reach the ropeworks just as a British soldier marches in.

Turn the page.

The soldier asks for a job. It's not unusual for soldiers to look for work in town. They are always short of money.

"You can clean the outhouse," one of the ropeworkers yells at the soldier.

The soldier's face turns as red as his coat. "Clean it yourself!" he yells back. The shouting match soon turns into a fistfight, but the soldier is outnumbered when the other workers join in.

"You'll be sorry you insulted me," the soldier says as he runs out the door. "I'll be back, and I won't be alone."

Sam walks over to say hello. "Nice to meet you," he says to you. "But you both should leave. It's too dangerous here."

Soldiers and townspeople clashed in the days before the Boston Massacre.

You think that Sam's probably right.

But Sarah's not worried. She wants to stay.

→ To leave, turn to page **88**.

→ To stay, turn to page **89**.

Cook is pleased that you've decided to stay and help her watch the house. You are both in the kitchen having a cup of Labrador tea when a message arrives for you from your father: "Mother is very ill. Come home."

You know right away that you must go. Your mother is expecting a baby soon. You hope that she'll be all right.

Mr. Hancock loans you a horse. By the time you reach Lexington, Mother is dying. She had a difficult time giving birth to your baby sister.

You bend down to speak with Mother. She takes your hand and whispers, "Promise me you'll take care of the baby."

"Yes, of course." You'd promise anything if it would help. But nothing you can say or do saves her life. She slips from sleep to death later that afternoon.

After her simple funeral, you tell your father, "I promised Mother I'd take care of baby Jane."

"Then go back to Boston," he says. You understand what he means. Your 12-year-old sister Molly can watch the baby, but she can't earn money to help support the family. You've been sending your pay home, and you know the family needs it. But what about the promise you made to your mother?

→To return to Boston, turn to page **90**.

→To stay in Lexington, turn to page **94**.

"We should go," you tell Sarah. A few minutes later, the soldier returns with several other soldiers. Ropeworkers armed with clubs are there to meet them.

"You don't want to get in the middle of this," Sam tells Sarah. You and Sarah leave the ropeworks just as the fight begins.

When Sarah stops by on Sunday night, she tells you that the fighting isn't over. "The soldiers came back for another fight on Saturday. Sam says we'll get even one way or the other. Tomorrow night, if the church bells ring, it will mean trouble."

Monday night around 9:00, the church bells do begin to ring.

➤To run outside, turn to page **91**.

➤To stay inside, turn to page **97**.

As you walk out the door, the soldier returns with several of his friends. You and Sarah duck into the alley. "At least we can see them without being in the middle of the fight," you say. The ropeworkers use clubs to hold off the soldiers. But as the soldiers leave, they yell that they'll be back.

You return to work at Mr. Hancock's. It's a tense weekend in Boston. Soldiers interrupt church services. Everyone seems nervous.

Around 9:00 on Monday night, March 5, the church bells begin to ring. "It's a fire!" Cook yells.

You grab a bucket to help fight the fire. But Cook holds you back. "What if it's not a fire? I have a bad feeling. I think you should stay inside."

→To run outside, turn to page **91**.

→To stay inside, turn to page **97**.

In a shipbuilding city like Boston, much activity centered around the wharf and harbor.

Your brother, Thomas, returns to Boston with you. He hopes to find a job there too. You reach Mr. Hancock's house on Monday, March 5. Thomas heads to the wharf to look for a job.

By nightfall, Thomas still hasn't returned. You worry that he's become lost. At 9:00, the church bells ring. That usually means a fire. Normally, you would go help fight the fire. But maybe you should wait in case Thomas returns.

To go outside, turn to page **98**.

To wait at the house, turn to page **99**.

You race outside. A large crowd is gathered in the street. You follow the crowd to King Street. Everyone is yelling and shouting. Young boys are throwing pebbles and snowballs at the soldiers. "Stand off!" the soldiers yell.

People in the crowd are taunting the soldiers. "Fire!" they yell. "Fire your guns!"

Boom!

A man near you cries out. Edward Payne, standing in the entry door of his shop, grabs his arm. "I've been shot."

You help him inside, where his wife binds the wound to stop the bleeding. "Please find a doctor," she begs.

Turn the page.

You dash outside to find the doctor. People are yelling, shouting, and pushing one another. Church bells clang. The streets are dangerous. You should get back to Mr. Hancock's house as quickly as possible. But Mr. Payne needs help.

→ *To return home, go to page* **93**.

→ *To run for the doctor, turn to page* **96**.

You turn and run as fast as you can toward Mr. Hancock's house. You feel bad about not getting the doctor for Mr. Payne. But with people being shot in the streets, you could be next.

You're panting by the time you reach Mr. Hancock's door. As you slip inside, Cook is there to meet you.

Turn to page 97.

"But I promised Mother that I'd stay and look after the baby," you say.

Your father doesn't say anything for a minute. You know he's thinking about Mother. "Well, maybe you're right," he finally says. "Caring for a baby is too much for Molly. There's plenty of chores to keep both of you busy."

You are shopping in Lexington when you hear about the Boston Massacre. On March 5, a group of British soldiers fired into a crowd of townspeople. Eleven men were shot, and five of them died.

"You could have been killed in that terrible city," your father says.

"Boston's a fine city if it weren't for the British troops," you say. "We should have the right to make our own laws here in the colonies."

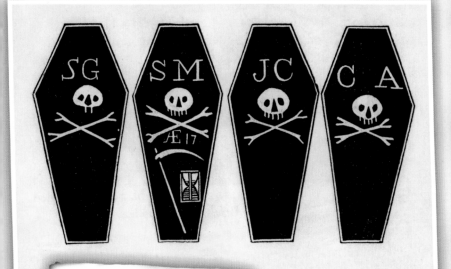

The coffins of the first four massacre victims were labeled with their initials.

"Someday, we may have that right," Father replies. "But until then, you made the right decision to leave Boston."

THE END

To follow another path, turn to page 11.
To read the conclusion, turn to page 101.

To follow another path, turn to page 11.
To read the conclusion, turn to page 101.

Samuel Adams (right, pointing) called for British troops to leave Boston.

You run for the doctor. "You're needed at Mr. Payne's," you say. He dashes off in that direction.

96

When you return home, everyone gathers around as you tell your tale. Even Mr. Hancock listens intently. "I've met with the other leaders of the Sons of Liberty," he tells you. "Tomorrow, we're demanding that the soldiers leave Boston."

THE END

To follow another path, turn to page 11.
To read the conclusion, turn to page 101.

Cook locks the door as the bells stop ringing. "Maybe the worst is over," she says. A short while later, there's a knock on the door. It's Sarah, in tears. There's blood on her cape. "Are you hurt?" you ask.

"It's Sam," she cries. "He's been killed by the British soldiers." Cook fixes Sarah a cup of Labrador tea, and you try to comfort her.

Between sobs, Sarah tells you the story. "Sam and the others threatened the soldiers, but only with words. Sam wasn't even armed. Some of the apprentices threw rocks and snowballs, and someone yelled, 'Fire!' Now Sam's gone forever. I hope to see those soldiers hang."

THE END

To follow another path, turn to page 11.
To read the conclusion, turn to page 101.

97

You run out to join the crowd. You're pushed along toward the Custom House on King Street.

You stand at the back of the crowd. About 100 people are shouting and throwing rocks and ice at a small group of soldiers. One man yells, "Fire! I dare you." A moment later, a gun goes off. Then you hear several more shots.

The crowd moves back. The bodies of the dead and wounded lie in the snowy street. You race for home. Thomas is waiting for you in the kitchen. You rush into his arms, sobbing.

Later, you learn five men were killed. "What if it had been you?" you ask Thomas.

"They died for the cause of liberty," he says. "Many more may die before the battle is won."

THE END

To follow another path, turn to page 11.
To read the conclusion, turn to page 101.

You wait at Mr. Hancock's house for Thomas. Is he lost? When you hear gunshots in the distance, you panic. What if he's been shot?

You dash into the street, but there is no sign of Thomas. You run toward the noise. Thomas staggers toward you. He has blood on his shirt. "Trouble on King Street," he gasps. "I was on my way here when soldiers started shooting into a crowd. A man standing beside me fell. I'm not sure if he was dead or just wounded. Others were shot as well."

"But you're not hurt?" you ask.

"No. I'm fine. But we can't stay here. Boston is a dangerous place. Tomorrow, we'll go back to Lexington, where all will be peaceful."

THE END

To follow another path, turn to page 11.
To read the conclusion, turn to page 101.

Samuel Adams (left) met with British
governor Thomas Hutchinson (right)
after the massacre.

CHAPTER 5

Aftermath of the Massacre

At the time of the Boston Massacre, Massachusetts law included the Riot Act. This law allowed police to break up a gathering of 12 or more armed people or 50 or more unarmed people. To do this, police read the Riot Act to the crowd.

On the night of March 5, 1770, no one read the Riot Act. Townspeople were then within their rights to gather in the streets.

But the townspeople weren't blameless, either. The soldiers held their tempers and their guns despite the crowd's taunting. But at some point, the soldiers thought they heard Preston give an order to shoot. That's when they opened fire. Crispus Attucks, Samuel Gray, and James Caldwell were killed at the scene. Patrick Carr and Samuel Maverick were wounded and died later. Edward Payne, Christopher Monk, John Clark, John Green, Robert Patterson, and David Parker were wounded but recovered.

After the Massacre, Boston's leaders demanded that the troops leave Boston. On March 6, acting governor Thomas Hutchinson asked the army commanding officer to move the troops to Castle William. This fort was on an island in Boston Harbor. During the next week, the troops were moved to the crowded fort.

After the shootings, the Sons of Liberty gathered eyewitness reports. Paul Revere distributed his famous engraving of the events. Revere wasn't there, but he based his engraving on a drawing by Henry Pelham. Word of the shootings spread throughout the colonies.

Captain Preston and the soldiers remained in prison awaiting trial. Boston lawyers John Adams and Josiah Quincy agreed to represent the men. Boston's leaders were eager to prove that Boston supported justice and fairness for all.

Preston's trial lasted from October 24 to October 30, 1770. John Adams pointed out that the witnesses did not agree on what happened. The jurors found Preston not guilty.

In late November, the other soldiers went on trial. The jury found six of the soldiers not guilty. These soldiers immediately returned to Great Britain. The jury found Hugh Montgomery and Matthew Killroy guilty of manslaughter. They were branded on their thumbs and sent back to Britain.

No one knows exactly what happened on the night of March 5, 1770. There was much confusion, and witnesses told different stories. But the event remains an important part of American history. Samuel Adams said that the Boston Massacre laid the foundation for American independence.

On April 19, 1775, the first battles of the Revolutionary War were fought in Lexington and Concord, Massachusetts. On July 4, 1776, members of the Second Continental Congress adopted the Declaration of Independence.

Many bloody battles followed until the British surrendered in October 1781. On September 3, 1783, the war officially ended with the signing of the Treaty of Paris. At last, the United States of America was a free and independent country.

On April 19, 1775, American soldiers won the first battles of the Revolutionary War.

TIME LINE

October 1, 1768 — British troops arrive in Boston.

February 22, 1770 — Ebenezer Richardson shoots and kills Christopher Seider.

February 26, 1770 — About 2,000 people attend Seider's funeral.

March 2 and 3, 1770 — Soldiers and ropeworkers fight at Gray's Ropeworks.

March 5, 1770 — British soldiers clash with patriots in several areas of Boston. At the Custom House, Boston residents Crispus Attucks, Samuel Gray, and James Caldwell are shot and killed. Samuel Maverick, Patrick Carr, Edward Payne, and five other men are wounded.

March 6, 1770 — Maverick dies; Captain Thomas Preston is arrested; eight other soldiers turn themselves in; patriot leaders demand that troops leave Boston.

March 10–14, 1770 — British troops are sent to Castle William in Boston Harbor.

March 14, 1770 — Patrick Carr dies, bringing the number of victims to five.

April 1770 — Ebenezer Richardson is found guilty of murdering Christopher Seider, but is later pardoned.

October 30, 1770 — Captain Preston is found not guilty.

December 5, 1770 — Six soldiers are found not guilty. Two are convicted of manslaughter.

December 16, 1773 — Patriots protest the tea tax during the Boston Tea Party.

April 19, 1775 — The Battles of Lexington and Concord are the first battles of the Revolutionary War.

July 4, 1776 — Members of the Second Continental Congress adopt the Declaration of Independence.

September 3, 1783 — The Revolutionary War officially ends; the United States of America is an independent country.

OTHER PATHS
TO EXPLORE

In this book, you've seen how the events surrounding the Boston Massacre look different from three points of view.

Perspectives on history are as varied as the people who lived it. You can explore other paths on your own to learn more about what happened. Seeing history from many points of view is an important part of understanding it.

Here are some ideas for other Boston Massacre points of view to explore:

+ At the time of the Boston Massacre, slavery was legal in the colonies. What would it be like to be a slave in a country that is fighting for its freedom?

+ Not everyone in the colonies supported the Sons of Liberty. What would it be like to be loyal to Great Britain during that time?

+ People living in Great Britain likely didn't understand why the colonists were angry. If you were living in Britain at that time, how would you have reacted?

READ MORE

Burgan, Michael. *The Boston Massacre*. Graphic History. Mankato, Minn.: Capstone Press, 2006.

Ready, Dee. *The Boston Massacre*. Let Freedom Ring. Mankato, Minn.: Bridgestone Books, 2002.

Santella, Andrew. *The Boston Massacre*. Cornerstones of Freedom. New York: Children's Press, 2004.

Walsh, Kieran. *Samuel Adams*. Discover the Life of a Colonial American. Vero Beach, Fla.: Rourke, 2005.

INTERNET SITES

FactHound offers a safe, fun way to find Internet sites related to this book. All of the sites on FactHound have been researched by our staff.

Here's how:

1. Visit *www.facthound.com*
2. Choose your grade level.
3. Type in this book ID **1429620129** for age-appropriate sites. You may also browse subjects by clicking on letters, or by clicking on pictures and words.
4. Click on the **Fetch It** button.

FactHound will fetch the best sites for you!

GLOSSARY

apothecary (uh-PAH-thuh-care-ee) — a drugstore

apprentice (uh-PREN-tuhs) — someone who learns a trade or craft by working with a skilled person

barracks (BEAR-uhks) — housing for soldiers

effigy (E-fuh-jee) — a dummy made to look like a hated person

import (IM-port) — to bring goods into one country from another

manslaughter (MAN-slaw-ter) — the crime of killing another person without intending to do so

militia (muh-LISH-uh) — a group of volunteer citizens who serve as soldiers in emergencies

musket (MUHSS-kit) — a gun with a long barrel

parliament (PAR-luh-muhnt) — people who have been elected to make laws in some countries

patriot (PAY-tree-uht) — a person who sided with the colonies during the Revolutionary War

repeal (ri-PEEL) — to officially cancel something, such as a law

sentry (SEN-tree) — a guard

BIBLIOGRAPHY

Bobrick, Benson. *Angel in the Whirlwind: The Triumph of the American Revolution.* New York: Simon and Schuster, 1997.

Forbes, Esther. *Paul Revere and the World He Lived In.* Boston: Houghton Mifflin, 1942.

Hansen, Harry. *The Boston Massacre: An Episode of Dissent and Violence.* New York: Hastings House, 1970.

Maier, Pauline. *From Resistance to Revolution: Colonial Radicals and the Development of American Opposition to Britain, 1765–1776.* New York: Knopf, 1972.

Polk, William Roe. *The Birth of America: From Before Columbus to the Revolution.* New York: HarperCollins, 2006.

Zobel, Hiller B. *The Boston Massacre.* New York: W. W. Norton, 1970.

INDEX